Dave Matthews Band

crash

Piano/Vocal Arrangements by John Nicholas

Cover Illustration by Thane Kerner
Band photography by C. Taylor Crothers

 *For a comprehensive listing of Cherry Lane Music's songbooks, sheet music,
instructional materials, videos and more, check out our entire catalog on the Internet.
Our home page address is: http://www.cherrylane.com*

Contents

Left to right: Leroi Moore (saxophones), Boyd Tinsley (violin), Carter Beauford (drums/percussion), Stefan Lessard (bass), Dave Matthews (guitar/vocals)

Dave Matthews Band

crash

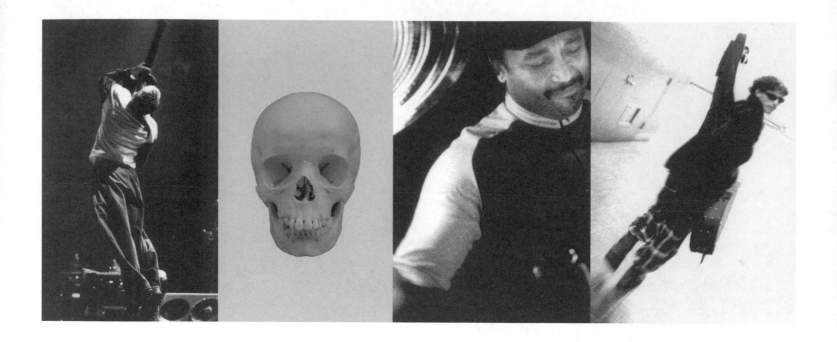

One of pop's most striking recent success stories has been the rise of the Dave Matthews Band, whose major-label debut *Under The Table And Dreaming* was praised by *Rolling Stone* as "one of the most ambitious releases of '94." The album has sold over four million copies, and earned two Grammy nominations for the first single, "What Would You Say."

The band was destined for such a breakthrough, with or without a Top 40 hit, thanks to its feverish grassroots support and the group's own unique talent. Dubbed "unpeggable and totally addictive" by *Details*, the Dave Matthews Band stood out from the horde of would-be alternatives with one of the most original sounds to emerge in the '90s.

Now the band is poised to break down more doors with *Crash*, its highly-anticipated second RCA album. "It's way more aggressive, way more sexy, way softer and way louder," says frontman Dave Matthews. For all its extremes, however, the diverse elements of Matthews' hypnotic voice and acoustic guitar, Boyd Tinsley's Cajun-spry violin, Leroi Moore's shy R&B sax, Stefan Lessard's funk-fluid bass, and Carter Beauford's power-jazz drums are broadened and blended into a more integrated, accessible form. From the funk-wound nerve of the first single, "Too Much," to the lusty ripples of "Crash Into Me," the Dave Matthews Band only sound more like itself.

Matthews credits producer Steve Lillywhite (U2, Talking Heads, Rolling Stones) with a relaxed, yet adventurous attitude in the studio. All band members played together to record the basic tracks. "We were more or less in a circle where we could all see each other," Matthews says of the sessions. "That makes this album a lot more in the spirit of how we play on stage."

There was a good deal of experimentation in the studio, too. Lessard brought a six-string and an acoustic bass into the mix. Moore added some funky baritone sax riffing to his arsenal, which he laid upon the other saxophone tracks of "So Much To Say." Moore also featured flute on "Say Goodbye," which opens with an amazing drum roll by Beauford, who contrasts his usual whiplash beats and fills with tasty percussion from congas, cowbells and woodblocks.

Tinsley also adopts a more textural role on violin, lacing "Two Step" with plucky pizzicato lines, while serving a familiar rustic rave-up in "Tripping Billies." That song, its name inspired by a girl-friend who said it sounded like "hillbillies on acid," was first heard on the group's self-released live debut, *Remember Two Things* (which has sold 350,000 copies since its 1993 release), but lost nothing in studio translation. "Boyd would start sawing away on his violin, and we were screaming and dancing and clapping around behind him," Matthews says of the new version. "When I hear that solo, it holds a big memory for me."

Indeed, the momentum and moods throughout much of *Crash* are the stuff of memories and hindsight, from the hairpin grooves of "Drive In Drive Out" to resonate low songs like "Let You Down." The sense that we are all primates—with simple goals cast to destiny—surfaces in the closing track, "Proudest Monkey," which Matthews relates to his own humble start as a bar-tender in Charlottesville, Virginia. "When the song started out, it was about how we people have sort of left, or at least like to think that we've left the woods," he says. "But I'm proud of the position that we've moved into."

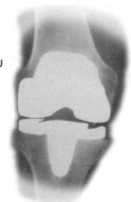

So Much To Say

Words and Music by David Matthews,
Boyd Tinsley and Peter Griesar

and I'm al-right._____ Yeah, yeah,_____ yeah._____

Can't_____ see the light. Keep it___ locked up in-side.___

_____ Don't talk_____ a-bout it._____ T-T-Talk a-bout the weath-er._____

Yeah, yeah,_____ yeah._____ Can't___

Fsus2 Dm G

— see the light. O - pen — up my head — and — let — me

Am   A   Fsus2

out, — — — a - lit- tle ba - by. — 'Cause here we have been stand- ing for a

Dm   G   Am

long,   long, — time. —

Fsus2   Dm   G   Am

Tread- ing trod - den trails for a long, long, — time. —

Two Step

Words and Music by
David Matthews

'cause life is short but sweet for cer - tain. Hey, we're climb - ing two by two. To be sure these days con - tin - ue, things we can - not

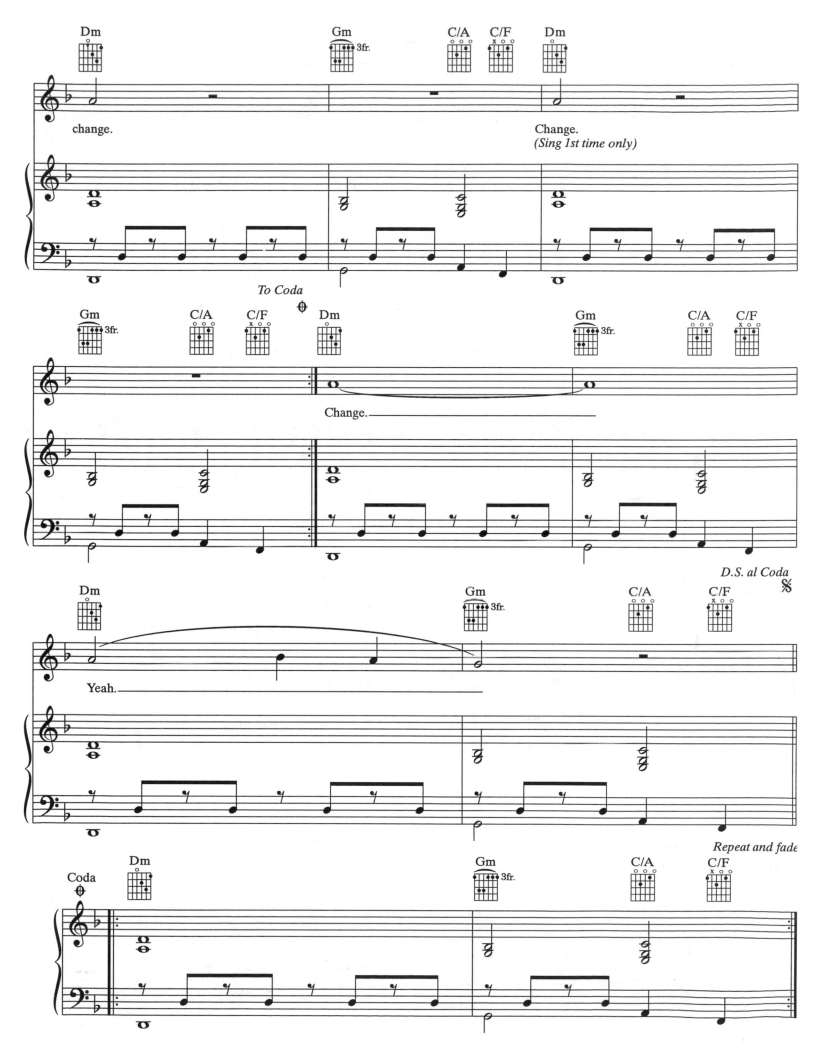

Too Much

Words by David Matthews
Music by David Matthews, Carter Beauford,
Stefan Lessard, Leroi Moore and Boyd Tinsley

Hmm, push it through the doors 'cause in between the lines

I'm gon-na pack more lines so I can get down in.

F#5

2. Oh, traf-fic jam, got more cars than a beach got sand.
3.4. *See additional lyrics*

Suck it up, suck it up, suck it up. Fill it up un-til no more. I'm no cra-zy creep.

you nev-er know,_____ may - be_____ you're__ dream - ing.

Coda I

F#5

Suck it up,___ suck it up, suck it up.

Suck it up, suck it up, suck it up, suck it up, ba - by.

'Cause I eat_ too much._ 'Cause I drink_ too much._

'Cause I want_ too much._____

F#5

Too much!

Repeat and fade

Additional Lyrics

2. Who do you think you're watching?
Who do you think you need?
Play for me, play more,
Ten times in the same day.
I need more.
I'm going over my borders.
Gonna take more,
More from you, letter by letter. *(To Chorus)*

3. I told God, "I'm coming to your country.
I'm going to eat up your cities,
Your homes, you know."
I've got a stomach full.
It's not a chip on my shoulder.
I've got this growl in my tummy
And I'm gonna stop it today. *(To Chorus)*

Crash Into Me

Words and Music by
David Matthews

1. You've— got your ball,— you've got your chain——— tied——

in a boy's dream.

Oh,

hike up your skirt a lit-tle more and show the

Additional Lyrics

3. Only if I've gone overboard,
   Then I'm begging you
   To forgive me, oh,
   In my haste.
   When I'm holding you so, girl,
   Close to me.
   Oh, and you come... *(To Chorus)*

#41

Words by David Matthews
Music by David Matthews, Carter Beauford,
Stefan Lessard, Leroi Moore and Boyd Tinsley

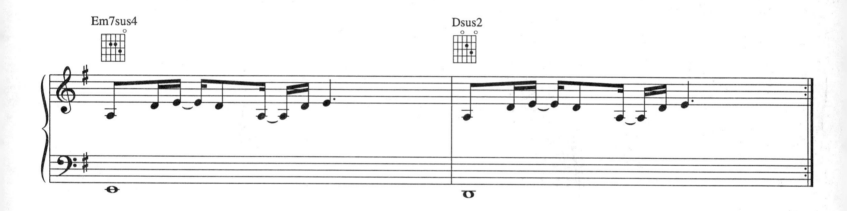

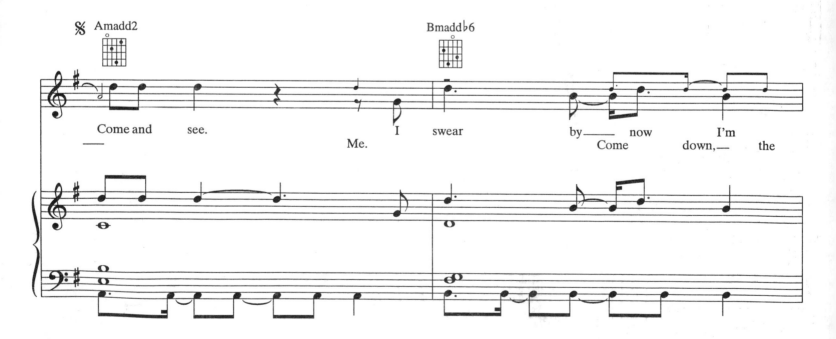

Come and see. Me. I swear by now I'm Come down, the

41

Say Goodbye

Words and Music by
David Matthews

bright. (1.) Oh,— and in your eyes I see— what's on— my—
2. *See additional lyrics*

— mind.— And you got— me wild,— turned a-round in-

side. And oh,— and then— de-si - re, see,— is creep-ing up heav-
(2.)3. *See additional lyrics*

y, ah, in - side here,———— and the way I

To - mor - row _____ say _____ good-

bye.

Additional Lyrics

2. Oh, go back to being friends,
   But tonight let's be lovers.
   We kiss and sweat.
   We'll turn this better thing
   To the best
   Of all we can offer.
   Oh, this rogue kiss,
   Tangled tongues and lips.
   See me this way.
   I'm turnin' and turnin' for you.
   Girl, just tonight. *(To Chorus)*

3. Oh, go back to being friends.
   Tonight let's be lovers.
   Oh, please, tonight let's be lovers.
   Say ya will, tonight let's be lovers.
   Oh yeah, tonight let's be lovers.

   3rd Chorus:
   And hear me call
   Soft-spoken, whispering love.
   A thing or two I have to say here.
   Tonight, let's go all the way, then,
   Love, I'll see you just for an evening.
   Let's strip down, trip out at this.
   One evening all starts with a kiss.
   And away... *(To Coda)*

Let You Down

Words by David Matthews
Music by David Matthews and Stefan Lessard

me pick you up._____ I let you

down._____ Let me climb____ up you____

____ to the top so____ I can see the view____ from

up there,_____ tan -

gled in your hair._____

I let you down._____

_____ I have no lid up - on_____

_____ my head,_____ but if I _____ did, you could look

I let you down. _____

I'm a pup – py for your love.

I'm a pup – py for your _____ love. _____

Additional Lyrics

2. I let you down.
   How could I be such a
   Fool like me?
   I let you down.
   Tail between my legs.
   I'm a puppy for your love.
   I'm a puppy for your love.
   I have no lid upon my head, *etc.*

Lie In Our Graves

Words by David Matthews
Music by David Matthews, Carter Beauford,
Stefan Lessard, Leroi Moore and Boyd Tinsley

way.
(Sing 1st time only)

To Coda

D.S. (with repeat) al Coda

When I'm

70

I can't be - lieve that we would

lie in our graves_____ won - d'ring if we _____ had spent our_____

_____ liv - ing days_____ well. I can't be - lieve that we would

lie in our graves,_____ dream - ing of things_____ that_____ we

might have been. Would_____ you

Cry Freedom

Words and Music by
David Matthews

Lyrics under first system: ter, go danc - ing through my head,— hu - man— as to— hu - man.— The fu-

Lyrics under second system: ture is— no place— to place your— bet - ter— days.—

Additional Lyrics

2. There was a window,
   And by it stood a mirror
   In which he could see himself.
   He thought of something,
   Something he had never had
   But hoped would come along.
   Cry freedom, cry,
   From deep inside,
   Where we are all confined.
   While we wave hands in fire, yeah. *(To Chorus)*

3. In this room stood a little child.
   And in this room, this little child,
   She would remain until someone
   Might decide to dance this
   Little child across this hall
   Into a cold, dark space,
   Where she might never trace her
   Way across this crooked mile,
   Across this crooked page.
   Cry freedom, cry,
   From deep inside,
   Where we are all confined. *(To Chorus)*

Tripping Billies

Words and Music by
David Matthews

We were a- bove, you were stand- ing un- der- neath us. We
We're wear- ing noth- ing, noth- ing but our shad- ows. Shad- ows
We are all sit- ting, legs crossed, 'round a fire.

Proudest Monkey

Words by David Matthews
Music by David Matthews, Carter Beauford,
Stefan Lessard, Leroi Moore and Boyd Tinsley

all— in a— day's— dream.— I am stuck like the oth - er mon - keys here.

I— am— a— hum - ble— mon - key,— sit - ting up in here,— a - gain.— 2. But then came the

day_____ I_ climbed_ out_ of these_ safe limbs,_

3. *See additional lyrics*

ven - tured_ a - way,_____ walk-ing tall,_ head_high up_ and_

sing - ing. I went to_ the cit - y,_____

car_ horns, cor- ners and the grit - ty._____ Now_ I__ am_ the

90

proud- est mon - key _____ you've ev- er seen.___

Mon- key see, mon-key do, yeah.___

1.

2.

Repeat and fad

3. Then comes the

Additional Lyrics

3. Then comes the day.
Staring at myself, I turn
To question me.
I wonder, do I want
The simple, simple life
That I once lived in well.
Oh, things were quiet then.
In a way, they were the better days.
But now I am the proudest monkey
You've ever seen.
Monkey see, monkey do.
Monkey see, monkey do.

Drive In Drive Out

Words and Music by
David Matthews

boil_____ my head_____ in a sense of____ hu -

mor. I laugh_____ at what I____ can - not____

____ change._____ And I throw it

all____ on the pile a - gain._____ And

93

beg, you___ a - void___ me.___

Be - cause I___ smell of dirt,___ hun - gry,___

hun - gry boy.___

You___ won't___ leave___ me all___ a -

98

Coda II

N.C.

Play 4 times

G

Additional Lyrics

2. Ooh, my head is pounding now.
   God has all but left me behind.
   Not a note of worry,
   I'm going to drive in and drive out again. *(To Chorus)*

3. Here, oh, I'm over this arrangement.
   Around here, emptiness sounded so good.
   I want to drive you right into my world. *(To Chorus)*

Cherry Lane
Music

• Quality In Printed Music •